I0141926

Maroon Daydreams

Cheyenne Raine

Content Warning: Some of the poems in this book discuss sexual abuse. Practice self-care or skip sensitive poems while reading this book.

© 2022 Raine and Rose Co. and Cheyenne Raine. All rights reserved.

ISBN-13: 978-0-578-38776-5

No part of this book may be reproduced, distributed, or transmitted by any means without prior consent of the publisher or author, except in brief quotations in reviews.

"Like the smell of burning sage in the morning, Cheyenne's words find a way to heal parts of you only good medicine can reach."

- Robert Harold Bordeaux,
Sicangu Lakota, author and activist

"Maroon Daydreams is a moving poetry collection that makes great, unknowable things into something soft that you can hold in your hands. While weaving through moonlight, I felt tenderly held by the author, and felt her pain in such a way that I knew I would also be healed in the end. The strength that radiates from this collection is astounding."

- Shelby Eileen, author of
Soft in the Middle

"Raine is incredibly talented at crafting powerful poems with tenderness. Her thoughts on the recovery process will empower you to heal in whatever way is best for you. This collection will make you think, leave you breathless, bring tears to your eyes and then put a smile on your face."

- Shelby Leigh, author of
changing with the tides

"This was an absolutely stunning collection of poems. The way Raine describes both hurt and healing is so haunting and real; beautiful and tragic in the most relatable way. This is a true work of art that will touch you and stay on your mind for many days after reading"

- Ida-Sofia, founder of
Evil Queen, shopevilqueen.com

"Maroon Daydreams is a battle cry. These poems are an expression of longing; a desire to be held and to hold. Cheyenne dives into the depths of humanity in its darkest moments; asking questions such as 'When you're alone— what does it feel like?' Knowing there won't be an answer, only more questions. Using vibrant imagery, the author also unravels the process of healing and its many stages, always moving toward wholeness and contentment."

- William Bortz, author of
THE GRIEF WE'RE GIVEN

This is for my hurt and your healing. This is something tender for us both.

Foreword

by Theresa Sopko Ressa, author of
Bewilderments of the Eyes

When I first dipped my toes into the
online poetry community, I was feeling
out whether or not I belonged, whether
I could actually write a poetry collection,
and I found a sea of artists who were
taking their words into their own hands
and dictating the ways in which they
would be heard and seen. These poets
were sharing pieces of themselves—
brazenly and unapologetically— they
were being uplifted by their fellow
creatives. I was mesmerized, and I
desperately wanted in. I began to see one
poet in particular over and over, both in
others' comments showing support, and
sharing some of the most gorgeous
words on her own page. That was
Cheyenne Raine.

Cheyenne was one of the first poets to
reach out to me. I was tentatively
sharing my own rickety poems, and she

was a constant beacon of encouragement and inspiration. When Cheyenne engages with others, she does so sincerely and with consideration. She reads between the lines and grasps the intangible, nuanced truths that are somehow the most essential. The vibrations and intuitions that you yourself can never seem to put into words, but recognize instantly, resonate so thoroughly within Cheyenne's work. Her writing is infused with sincerity and consideration. A natural mastery of the in-between. She strings together words and sentences that produce sound and feeling and experience. The culmination is almost a physical touch, something that nudges you along and whispers, "Pay attention. Feel. Grow."

In the time when I was wading in the shallows of poetry and its community, *Maroon Daydreams* was a revelation. As a collection, *Maroon Daydreams* is forgiving in the most tremendous way— it eradicates shame in healing. Lyrical and lilting, *Maroon Daydreams* is a mastery of endurance and indulgence. After a few years, I've grown to know and cherish Cheyenne as a friend and have grown a business alongside her. She continues to persevere, with an iron will and a strong desire to uplift others and provide the resources poets need to be heard. Our vision and mission statement for Raine and Rose Co. alone speaks to her sense of cultivation and tenderness.

Cheyenne mentioned to me that she was working on revamping her debut poetry collection, and I received that news with stars in my eyes. How could *Maroon Daydreams*—a collection I am so fond of, a collection that opened my eyes to today's poetry—possibly be improved upon? I was eager to find out. And, in what I've come to learn is true Cheyenne fashion, the remastered edition of *Maroon Daydreams* is, again, a revelation. Despite how giddily I anticipated this book, I didn't realize the need I had for it until I was devouring it with a knife and fork. I wasn't at all surprised to find poems within these pages that spoke directly and boldly to me and my current season of life—or to once more be transported and calmed, left with a sense of direction, a sense of support in my own perseverance. Somehow, Cheyenne still knows exactly what I need to hear. This latest edition of *Maroon Daydreams* follows and widens its original footprints: simultaneously unrelenting and gentle, firm and unyielding even in its pondering and musing, a sometimes-difficult story with an open end— allowing for growth and light to carry on. It highlights the duality of living, the light and the dark. This collection is not a dismissal of the darkness or of the hurt. It is a confrontation and a hope that, while some darkness may be inevitable, so is light and beauty. It is a promise that both can exist at once.

The reason I dwell so much on Cheyenne the person as well as Cheyenne the poet is because there is no disconnect. Through all her growing and her healing and her continual evolution, she is unfailingly genuine. She pours only herself onto the page and is gracious enough to share it with us all. Cheyenne, as well as her works, offer an acknowledgement of self that can also be an acknowledgement of and call for community. As someone who exudes resilience and strength, and is always giving her time, her energy, and her gifts, Cheyenne is the moon incarnate, gently shedding light to both illuminate the trials and to guide you through them. As an extension of its author, *Maroon Daydreams* will take you along a necessary path, but it will not leave you to journey alone.

The Hurt
& Harbor

Healing Comes in Many Ways

I allow wildflowers to blossom
from the hollows
of my broken bones.

It Is Unwanted

A coldness creeps into my chest,
unwanted and unexpected.
like a disease that spreads
into my veins.
I am left with the goosebumps.
I am left with the trauma.
I am left alone.

This coldness is unsafe,
it teaches me to unlove.
It leaves me isolated.

(In a world where my trauma
is unwanted. unheard.)

The Mourning

Some days I mourn my innocence.
I mourn my childhood.
Some days I mourn my voice,
that it became too heavy—
it had to turn to ink.
sometimes, I don't have words
for the pain that swells up within
the wall of my ribcage.
It just hurts. and I no longer
sleep with pillows because
all they do is gather tears.
sometimes I wake up from nightmares
that drag me twenty steps backwards,
as if all this time has not passed.
as if it were the first trauma
all over again.
some days...

Some days the world is too heavy,
and I haven't the strength.

Cheyenne Raine

Thank You for Holding Me While I Was an Earthquake

This is me
curling into your arms.
This is me
admitting that I
am far from okay.
This is me
when I am hurt.

This is also me
allowing myself to crumble
into the earthquake.

A Poem on Being Tired of Saltwater

Today I cried because I was tired.
I was tired of counting the number of
tears it took to become a waterfall of
freshwater.
how many it took to reach the sea,
where and when healing could begin.

Sometimes
it's a year. ten years. three months.
A lifetime of steps forward
and steps back. the cycle,
the unwanted pull—swallowing
progress.

I was tired of explaining
why my. her. his. their. our pain
is more than a story and a truth,
why it was a revolution and a battle cry
to be heard. Because no one.
no one.
should have to feel this. carry this.
no one should have to know this.

Yet, we do.
we know it and live it,
and we are lucky if we are survivors.

we are lucky if we can rebuild.
Although... is it really luck?

Cheyenne Raine

Today I wept because it was too much,
it was too much of remembering
and no steps forward.

but I washed the saltwater against my
skin and wore it for the day. If anything,
I can at least wear my story.
I can at least use my lungs to grow my
voice.

Snow

Snowfall in the afternoon
with tears in my eyes
—will this be the swift wave of
mourning?
I can't hold this hurt for much longer,
it pours out of my laughter at times,
spills as the shower runs.

The weather is cold as I sit on the patio
and ask if the hurt needs to return.
If it stays like this.
maybe it will leave. maybe it inches its
way into the ground and becomes part of
the soil.
maybe something good takes root
and escapes from the earth.

I watch as the snowflakes
land between the curtains.
A cold evening
creeps into my arms, taking up space
that I reserve for the warmth life gives
to me by way of friends
that bring hot cocoa to me and curl up
beside me on the patio, talking about
their day
and how they hope tomorrow the snow
melts.

Cheyenne Raine

A Little Bit of Room

I just need time.
I just need sunlight.
I just need saltwater.
I just need healing.
        please, give me
        a little bit of room
        to recover.

Staying in Bed – *for Alex*

My bed swallows me whole.
and the blankets
stick to my chest.
cling to my limbs.
I do not even try
to roll over.
Maybe if I am still enough
(stiller than my lamp),
time will slow down and give me
the space I need—maybe,
my body will remember
that movement is good.
But, time does not hesitate.
the blankets become warmer
than the autumn sun.
For some reason, this is hard.
It is heavy and it does not fit
in my thoughts.
Yet, I am here.
and my chest rises and falls.
and my pulse flows.
and even though time
is a grandfather clock
chiming in my head,
there is also this bed
and it is waiting
for my body to take in
the deepest of breaths.

At Times I Wonder

Prayer is a practice
I haven't worked on.
God isn't in my words and hopes.
I think God is in the roses that
a friar brought to me. I think God is
in my son's laughter, my goodness,
his laughter is so loud, like mine.

He makes me laugh. He is always happy.
My sweet little human.

At times I wonder if God
is in my eyes. If my son will see
God in the love I gift to him each
morning.

This Existence of Mine

I draw little planets across my skin,
a reminder to myself that I am made
of unique and fascinating patterns.
I might have flaws, still the moon
has deep craters and shadows. doesn't
everyone continue to adore it, in all of its
chaotic existence?

Yes, I know they do. and, so,
I will learn to love this existence of
mine.
I will learn to love these bones and
this breath.

Have Mercy

I beg the moon to be merciful.
petals that drift down my cheeks
like strands of hair I tie back.

I pulled over in a parking lot
to cry. Moonlight pretending
to be tender for a moment.

The Truth Is That I Hate My Story

The truth is that I hate when people tell
me that there is a reason for everything.
that God / the universe gives you what
you can handle. I hate when they say
that this will make me stronger.
I hate when they say someone has
endured worse. The truth is that I did
not deserve what was done to me.

the universe did not tell him to rape me.
God did not tell him to abuse me. God /
the universe didn't make this happen.
it was a human. it was their fault.
(and sometimes people will make it seem
as if it were my fault. I hate that, too.)

The truth is that I wasn't sure if I could
handle my own story. I still choke up
when I share it. the truth is that I
shouldn't have to share such a story.

the truth is that I hate when people tell
me that I am stronger for having gone
through the abuse.

Cheyenne Raine

As important as the healing is,
I feel it's even more important
that people see it for what it is:

I shouldn't have to be
on this healing journey.
I shouldn't have to be stronger, in this
way.
I shouldn't have gone through this.
do not tell me otherwise.

This is my truth.

Have You Ever?

Have you ever tried
to swallow a lie
because the truth was too much?
Did it feel like broken glass
forcing its way down your throat?
Did it make your voice
rough around the edges and raspy?
Did the secret hurt
as it inched its way
into your belly?
did it give you nothing but pain?

I remember when I first
let honesty push past my lips.
I coughed up blood. but it came out
smoother than the lie. it was still hard
to speak, but it was powerful.
it didn't beg for shelter,
it wanted to taste the air.

Cheyenne Raine

A Breather

Give it time
and love.
Give yourself
a breather
and a second
to unwind.
Give it a moment
to become
something sweeter.

Peach Globe

The sun has kissed the sky
a small peach globe of light.
The moon crawls to the stars
and I feel safe.

Is safe when you intrude?
When you come out of your dark?
how you steal my night?
is safe when you violate
my sense of self?
my place of refuge?

— No. —

I own my deep blue.
my tiny sparkling golden dots.
my grey clouds with purple bellies.
my lamp posts that flicker.
my barefoot path on warm asphalt.
my bruised body. it is mine.

I own my healing, too.
and you are nothing but rust
on the side of a building
that no one visits.
deteriorating in exile.

I am a lighthouse.
fluorescent yellow dancing
above cold black waves.

Cheyenne Raine

My body is a bonfire
with ashes that stain the sky
with new beginnings.
I claim moonrise to moonset.
they are mine. my own.

I claim shadows and night creatures
—they soothe me.
you are nothing, really.
you see, you do not own
the night sky,
or the howling wolves.
you do not own the poison
in a snake's fangs or
the blanket of darkness.

The sun kissed my cheeks
when the moon began to slumber
and, guess what?
I am a tapestry of my own healing.

I Unravel with Her – *for*
Keyana

I've rested my head in his hands
hoping that I could be vulnerable.
It lasts a few seconds before
I return to myself.

I am constantly unraveling myself
with her, and I haven't even met her yet.
She lives over a thousand miles
away from me.
She lives with her plants and somehow
manages to tuck me into her shoulder
and thread her fingers through my hair
while she listens to my unfolding.

I want to gift her full moons,
and flowers that blossom in the
rainforests.
I want her to have a string of lights
on a little balcony in a city that sleeps
at two in the morning—the perfect time
for her to type notes up on her phone.
Phoebe Bridgers on a record player
that plays softly in her small kitchen.
A little place of her own that I can visit
often. often. often.

Cheyenne Raine

I want her to have a glow in her smile
as often as I can manage to give her joy.

I release my hurt into her hands
and she sends me a song to listen to.

The Ship That Sails

How the hell am I supposed to write
a poem about healing
when I shove these thoughts down
my throat like headache pills
I take when the weather changes
or I haven't eaten in seven or so hours.
Just busy, I tell myself, with hands
full of paperwork or typing away.
Too busy to care about all the hurt
I have been harboring.
A ship waiting to sail, tied to my bones.
Anchored to my fingertips.

I want to sail past this pain.

Cheyenne Raine

The Aloneness

When you're sitting on the balcony,
does it come back to you?
the aloneness, curling
tendrils around your shoulders.
(Your shoulders,
the ones that carry the phases
of the moon and the setting
of the sun.)

When you're alone ☿
what does it feel like?
would you tell me why it feels right,
why it feels necessary; counting
the number of heartbeats it takes
to point out five yellow things
and two blue things.

The Gift of an Aloe Vera

Mamá tried, you know?
she tried to plant lilies in my palms,
but I was too angry. too hurt.
I was full of grief. in mourning.
She tried to send soft blankets
and warm soups,
but I was too full of rage.
Where do I look to find a place
where the hurt will not be so loud?
Where it will not throb so often?

She tried, my mamá,
with her sweet lullaby words.
She ended up gifting me an aloe vera.
A tough little succulent that had
healing in between its folds.
Maybe that was her wish for me,
that my soul would remain strong,
but the healing would begin
in my veins.

Cheyenne Raine

Wool Sweaters

You were all wool sweaters
and thick cotton sleeves.
I was dry bones and
broken laughter.
You couldn't save me.
Yet, you stayed.
and I learned to
become stronger
for myself.

Before I Bite My Tongue

My hesitation falls out
of my mouth and lands
on hot pavement,
like sidewalk chalk
that children play games to.
the game of bravery.
What is it to be brave?
when hesitation leaves,
I am undressed
and dissected.
the sky cracked open
like a coconut, when the milk
of the moon spills out and
splashes against your face.

it is when I am going to bite
my tongue, but decide to
pull apart every syllable
and give them to you.
raw, untouched things.
my hesitation doesn't exist
when you collect reasons for me
to feel safe and brave with you.

Cheyenne Raine

Will the Storm Calm?

Do you think the storm
will tire of its cackling?

No, no I don't think it will.

It's been pouring for hours now.
The thunder has not let up.
Why hasn't it calmed?

*Sometimes
there is too much. so much.
and it doesn't know how
to stop the aching.
It doesn't know when
the pain will leave.
So it sheds too many tears.
so many raindrops.
and it chokes on its air,
and it mourns the sky.*

*Sometimes,
There's just too much
and it weeps all night long.*

Tell Me About the Sun

Tell me something good about the sun.
About the way it glistens across the
surface of the sea,
waves of honey
making their way
to reach your toes.
Tell me something good about the moon.
About the way it sheds light
across the sidewalks and roads,
while you spend your evenings
chasing thoughts that spin in your head.

Tell me something good about
wildflowers.
Maybe how they beg you to pause
and soak in the moment, especially in
Texas, with your windows down and
country music playing on your radio.
I enjoy you singing country songs.

Tell me something good about yourself.
Today you tried. Today you were good.
better. Today was soft and kind to you.

Tell me something good, because I need
to know that there's more out there than
the fear of visiting the beach alone.

Cheyenne Raine

Walking home alone at night.
pulling over in my car, alone, to enjoy
the wildflowers on an almost empty
highway.

Tell me that you'll understand
why I hesitate.

Why I need to know
that there is more good out there.
Tell me something good,
before I forget to remember
that good exists
for me, too.

Maybe I Am Still Hurting

Maybe
my fists are still clenched.

maybe
my stomach is still in knots.

maybe
my heart is still pumping too quickly.
My thoughts are still reeling
over the loss.
Today is still too difficult to manage.

maybe
today is more bad than good.

Yet, maybe, just maybe,
you call to tell me about
your sister convincing you
to get another tattoo and you
ask where my thoughts are.
You give me room to smile.
at least for this moment.

Where the Pain Is Rooted

I am trying to remember where the pain
rooted itself, nowadays
I can't seem to place
the ache of springtime.
It's always there, quiet. waiting.
this year, I think to myself,
this year I have to skip over it.
push it further into the earth so that
even the rain cannot give it life
for sprouting tears.

this year, I have to at least try.
building myself a memory
that feels better.
building a moment to feel safe in.

A Gentle Daydream

Tired Poems

I prefer sleepy. tired poems.
they have nothing to hide.

I like almost closed eyes
and barely awake words.
softly folded into palms
and warm blankets.

You like that I am good.
For you. For me. For us.
I like that, too.
It is sweet, oh, so sweet.
to be good, to feel good.
I like drowsy intentions and smiles
that taste like love. I like love.
Love is why I am good.
is why I like you. is how I write
and plant lullabies in your bones.
Sometimes, I wrap fragments of stories
into the patterns of your skin.

I like this,
this evening that dozes off
before I say goodnight.

Fluttering Wings

You have been anticipating the Summer,
the waves of heat falling
against her skin, someone to dive into,
someone to leave you full of life.

Little fluttering wings
dancing across your spine,
soft breaths in the air
and opening up
your soul: do you know
what it feels like
to kiss the sky
and chase fireflies?

Cheyenne Raine

Storytelling Is Magic

Magic is sitting down on my bed
and telling you a story about a bat
that drifted from its family
to live in a cave
where a strange formation of crystals
lit the ceiling every night.

A story about a fighter that was forced
to fight every day to sleep
on his bed and eat a meal, eventually
escaping and running until
his feet couldn't run anymore—
finding himself in a vast forest,
using his strength to build himself a
home
and live quietly. Still training,
afraid that one day he might be found.
A story that he passed peacefully,
in his little home of wood and hope.

A story about a dragon that would
dance in thunderstorms, causing the rain
to appear like silver and gold
falling against an abandoned castle.
A dragon whose only friend was a snake.

Crafted into Something, Like Wanting

I craft my hands into bird wings
that maybe take you into the clouds
where the sun glows in your brown eyes.

Motherhood is a season
I cannot outgrow
to be yours. to be yours
as long as the moon remains with us.

My little giant,
how close I hold you to me.
and beg for aloneness. Asleep beside me,
there is a quiet that is full. A gulp
of the sea in my lungs. your face
turns towards me in your sleep.
The only sound is you and I—waves
lapping against the walls.

I am still a woman with the word mamá
scribbled into my palms. Still a woman
with dreams and plans.
Dreams to adventure with you.
Plans to grow with you.
Still chasing after my own healing
and my own creativity.

Hiding you in my heart,
where love comes
to inspire my fingertips with light.

I craft my hands into a boat
that sails past the morning clouds,
slowly wanting more than this day.
Wanting more than the sun is able to
mouth into a crater.

Remember to Write This Down

The sky was grey and the morning
was stillness waiting for a sign to move.
the windows were open, droplets falling
against the carpet and into the curtains.

On the couch, a book still in hand,
she is tucked into a story that she
fell asleep reading, all I can think to do is
to place another blanket on top of her
before I step out to the porch
to feel the rain against my face.
I'm all set to go, duffel bag in hand
and my gas tank full.

Remember to write this moment down,
will you? I want you to remember me
like this.

Cheyenne Raine

Like Atlas Does

If a poem refuses to slip
out of my mouth,
      what am I to do?
      Dive deep(er).
Saltwater pushes its way past my lips.
I gnaw on the remnants of a thought
as it tries to remind me
of my trauma. I, kindly, refuse
such a taste. I make my way
to the next wave from the sea.
a tall crest to sweep me away.

bravery is a thing
we have to learn.
it's a thing I intend to keep,
so I dive into uncharted waters.
When you land on the shoreline,
a grain of sand slips into the sea
for each speck of light
to touch your eyes.
I trace the lines on your skin,
maps to nowhere.
maps to a muscle. a bone.

I cannot hold the sky,
like Atlas holds the world.
It falls. it hides the clouds.
The rain comes and you are quiet.

Maroon Daydreams

If I could craft a spear
from sea glass and driftwood,
the sea would be yours to command.

Atlas wouldn't refuse.

Couldn't Be

The funny thing is that you aren't
holding me.
maybe you never did / it's just a fuzzy
memory that I can let go of now. 3am on
a couch with some vampire comedy
that still makes me laugh   but now
it's just the laughter
and your arms have disappeared
from the memory of watching the film
for the first time.   but now
it's just the midnight tires rolling to the
sound of Soundgarden and Pearl Jam
with no one singing but myself
and your voice never touched the air.

It's 11pm and I stayed in bed with
dreams of bats and spiders, you never
pressed call and asked me to pick you up
from the bar. you never asked how I
was.

and it's okay this way.
It'll be a distant thing.
something that never was. couldn't be.

Any and Every Place

Dizzy eyes spin
into cotton candy clouds,
you pick wildflowers
for the rearview mirror,
my worn-out jeans
lean against your faded walls.
String lights lead you
to any and every place.

A small street.
Anywhere, but home.

Dear Moon in a Lavender Sky

Dear moon,
(can you hear me?)
I am giving the light
back to you.

You wear it well,
better than I.
I tried, you see,
to be silver, whole,
crescent, pulling
at the ocean waves /
but, I do not know
how you do it
       all at once.

I give the light
back to you.
I'll sit on my porch
and admire you
in all your stillness.
hanging in a lavender sky.

I Want More

"I want more love," he tells me.
"I want a reason to throw the next
punch, a reason to rest.
a reason to pick up fresh flowers and add
cash to an orange mason jar labeled 'you
and I,' as I start to brainstorm ideas as to
where our next adventure could be.

"Hell, I want a love that reminds me
that working is not my life, that I should
call in and spend the weekend with you
by the shoreline or hiking. A love that is
climbing into the car for banana splits at
1am.

"I want to look at you when we're
arguing and think: why the hell are we
making so much noise? Come here and
slow dance with me. We can let this
misplaced anger go. I want more of us."

As You Are Unfolding, Always, I Adore You

The dust settles in crevices
found between branches,
little specks of light dripping,
like tree sap:

Warm honey.
Nectar from pale flowers.
Golden fingertips waiting
to brush the dust away,
waiting to uncover silver
that has been tucked away
in roots, for far too long.

A Dream of You

A dream of you,
playing who knows what
on your guitar,
while the sky tastes
like ripe raspberries.
A dream of you,
singing like the rain
falling over the desert,

gentle and welcomed.

Cheyenne Raine

The Sky in My Bedroom

Where the stars
have fallen—
twinkle and glitter across
the walls painted of grey,
my fingertips scrape the clouds,
hoping that the rain will return,
/ when it comes, it fills
the air with a gentleness
that has yet to be held.
I've begged for more nectar
to drip from the corners of my eyes
because I, too, want more
things that taste of honey
and sugarcoated words that sweeten
with time.

My tongue stays still, though,
and I must find a place / where
the waves could breathe,
I bite into a ripe peach
and wait for the light to unravel.

Stories Built in Moments
Like These – *for Gabriel*

I've been building stories, you see,
the kind where the sea splashes up
against the stone walls with a crashing
sound—the sound of the wind roaring
into an open window as your car rushes
down the highway.

The kind where sirens are lullabies
without fires and tears, without such
urgency, a lull,
my hand swaying from the edge
of the bed, where imagination begins
to doze off into dreams I vaguely recall.
like bathing in milk
or a tub full of roses.

Sometimes, I think these stories are
meant to stay in your eyes,
where the stars
do this funny thing, twirling around
and you are dazed. wandering far.
I've no map to reach you,
just a song that my palms
cannot carry for too long—

Cheyenne Raine

mostly,
we share this tiny speck of a second
when the moon is rubbing its eyes
and the sun is tossing about,
that is where I build the stories,
in these moments with you.

I think a part of you will always be lost,
the long nights
when everything is too quiet
but I take you with me
wherever I go, nothing is left behind,
perhaps you are just hidden, a shadow
resting its chin on a fingertip,
a warrior living in a castle made of
driftwood.

Into the Abyss

Black boots. black t-shirt. black pants.
black leather jacket. black leather gloves.
You drive off, in a cloud of dust, on your
motorcycle. the night wears you down,
listening to your thoughts on repeat,
like a favorite playlist.
Black hair and black eyes.
You fall into the abyss.
A storm rolls in and you are too far.

Cheyenne Raine

To Behold Life

Behold sounds like such a holy word,
to behold this experience
and feel it wrap around
every fiber of my being
so that it becomes a pulse and a melody.
Humming while the sun sets, light
playing with my hair, a ceiling fan
spinning
in sync with my heartbeat.

to behold the magic of living.
scribbling down poems about joy,
hurting, healing, and all the moments
between here and there.

A Thousand Ways to Open

You open your mouth
and flowers blossom
from your words.
You open your eyes
and galaxies burst
within your visions.
You open your heart
and love grows into
a thousand songs
to sing to the moon.

Cheyenne Raine

Half-Way to Motherhood

There is a little baby growing
in my belly.
Someone I could never imagine
knowing, it is beyond me.

Motherhood is terrifying, as it comes
with waves taller than the
crown of my head,
but my crown stays in its place
and reminds me that I am rooted
in the sea of becoming.

Motherhood is a few months away
and I still don't know how to feel.
there is excitement about baby laughs
and little hands
that will hold my fingertips
and tangle in my hair—in the purest of
ways, ways that remind me
of someone good
and their soft intentions in touching me.
touch. there it is.
Motherhood is touch—blowing bubbles
on my baby's belly to hear laughter.

At the end of the day (if there is an end)
I will have nothing but my songs
and my prayers, my tired and my messy.

This baby will gulp down gallons of my
love and will return it to me with fragile
kisses.

There is a seed of faith growing in my
belly's soul, knowing that the baby will
know Love.
Love that is God, Love that is Christ.

Love that is La Virgen de Guadalupe.
and my own mother,
she has parts of God in her, too.
maybe it is a part of motherhood.

When the time comes this unknowing
and insecurity will be shed
from my skin,
like a snake embracing its new scales.
Scales that shine with hope
and curiosity and light.
When I hold my baby will I feel it?
will the moon remind me
to soak in the light?

Cheyenne Raine

Half-way through my pregnancy and
being a mother is still foreign to me,
my tongue doesn't quite understand. my
skin stretches to make room.
This afternoon I placed my hand over
my belly and felt my baby kicking, it is
still so wild to think that another
heartbeat is so close to mine.

Open Highways

Open highways that wind
up and down the countryside,
pavement and hills all tangled up,
wind blowing in the trees—
letting your fingers
spread out under the sky,
      this road is yours.

Something Like Messy Sheets

Morning light with
a warm glass of tea,
something like messy sheets
and my hand in yours,
       something like snoozing
       all the alarm clocks
       and touching the folds
       of cotton sheets.

The Light That Drips

It is with great love
that I watch the stars fall out
from the strands of your hair,
light dripping like sap.
Softly landing on the ground.
It is with great love
that the night sky uncurls
from your hair, a sparkle
of bliss in your eyes.

Tucking your chin against my palm,
closing your eyes and sighing.
something so pure. someone so bright.

Cheyenne Raine

The City That Sings

My city sings itself to life every night,
a song of resilience and becoming.
This city that hardly makes time
for the winter.

I daydream
like I write,
thoughts of you
and I, running
between city lights.

My city twirls me into your song.
Holds me against the noise.
Carries me into the night.

This city I will leave, and always
find a reason to come back.

Your Palms Are a Nest for My Feather Heart

Little bird singing
from the top of a tree,
clueless to the weight
that gravity places
against my bones—
still, it sings and sings
and the song takes me
to a place I would never reach
if it weren't for gentle peach skies.

little bird, small in my hands.
like you, it sings,
I fit in your arms and you
hold me so close.

Cheyenne Raine

Cardboard Room

I live in a cardboard room,
where one slight drizzle causes my roof
to deteriorate. and the wind knocks
my walls over. It's far from sturdy.
reliable. safe. But it's mine. Complete
with pale green stars glued to the top.
A small cut out for a window to my left.

I pretend it's a home, you see?
A home for my pain. which is why
it falls apart at the slightest storm.
My story spilling at the seams.
It is not much of a home.
not much of a room.

What is it like to be ready?
To be so full of courage, the truth pours
out of your lips like bird wings in flight?
Is it like flying, where the wind does not
blow you down but lifts you up into
clouds that taste like fresh raspberries?
Does it mean that I will no longer have
this cardboard room?

I have so many questions. I have carried
this home with me, wherever I have
traveled. what if my story stays behind
the window? that would be alright,
wouldn't it?

I Bury the Grief

The tea kettle whistles to me
as I rush into the kitchen
to turn the stove off
and grab the nearest mug.

Sometimes I lose myself in a story
and forget the world outside of the living
room. Today the tea is a mixture of rose,
chamomile, and lemon.

The pages are a mixture of grief and
hope.

Tomorrow I will have caramel and chai.
I will write about the tea kettle and the
gift of a quiet afternoon to bury my
words into.

Brief Moments in this Life

Statistics and the Soul

In the United States, my nation, where
freedom is for all: I am one in every 6
women to know that the word rape is
more than a word.
I am where 55 percent of assaults
happen: at or near the home.

In Texas, my home, my state of blue
bonnets and barbeque:
I am one of 4.2 million women to
experience assault at some point in their
lifetime. I am twice as likely to be
assaulted because I am a woman. I am
27.9 percent of Latinas to experience
assault. I am one in 6 cases of assault to
be reported to law enforcement.

I am a statistic you read about.
breathing, here, before your eyes.
When I describe myself, I'll tell you
that I am a creative. I am a poet and
author.
I am a Latina and I was raised by a single
mamá who taught me to enjoy the sight
of sunflowers and always look for the
moon,
once the sun has set.
I enjoy horror movies and
I am a bookworm.

Cheyenne Raine

I am a tea enthusiast and
I love to listen to mariachis.

Right now, I will tell you that I am a
survivor.
I am healing. I am learning how to share
my story. I am an advocate for those
affected by sexual assault.
I am an advocate for healing from
trauma.
I hate hearing trauma stories, even my
own.

A word: trigger.
That's what I feel when I hear these
stories. when I read about them. I
mourn for those who know what I
mean. (Please, be gentle with yourself.
I'll be gentle with you, too.)

I mourn for those who almost know
what I mean, almost. because they
almost had to tell a story. or hold it in.

I am a survivor who found her voice, but
not many do. and even when they do,
sometimes they are told to be quiet. it's
not appropriate. they didn't have it that
bad. there are other issues in the world
that are more important.

I am a survivor, more than a statistic.
I have every reason to be angry, and I
am,
but I am also hurting and trying to bring
more light and more awareness and more
hope and more kindness into my
community.

You are my community.
I am a statistic you read about,
and I am your neighbor. your friend.
your family. your community.
A woman standing in front of you,
asking to be heard.

Statistics taken from the Rape, Abuse & Incest
National Network (RAINN) and the Texas
Statewide Sexual Assault Prevalence Study
(2015).

Balconies and Autumn Leaves

Over and over
I roll a beautiful word
around my tongue.

What makes sitting on the edge
of the balcony any better than
sitting at a bar, waiting for a beer?
What makes this word
so different? Is it the power
it holds (even when it is whispered
or moaned into the moonlight)?
Is it the clarity and kindness?

I feel so exposed. (Unearth
the roots of my soul, now.
Illuminating the ground below me.)
I let my laughter fall from my toes
like autumn leaves in a yellow sky.

In the Bed of a Truck – *for*
Ellie and Claudia

Do you remember the days
when we would talk nonsense
in the bed of a truck
while we were parked
under the sunset in a Texas sky?
I do. The stars in your eyes
kept me captivated.

It was perfect for Texas, the sound
of cars rushing by on I-35,
the scent of barbeque
drifting towards us,
and the heat sticking to us like honey.

Take Care

Take care, I tell you,
Take care—because the world outside
is unforgiving and cruel. because
the people wouldn't take kindly
to your outbursts of pain.
because society cannot hold you
like I do. Take care, I whisper,
because in this lifetime
you are still good.
You are still worthy.

Festival Lights

Festival lights
and carnival rides,
running through
the lines of people,
laughing at the sunset

— one ticket lets us sit
on top of the city view.

You Build Me a Dream

You take my healing and weave it into
the curtains that hang in front of the
windows, you take my laughter
and play it on speakers
sitting on the coffee table, you take my
dreams and cast them onto the TV,
you take my tears and use them to wash
away the pain.

Your thumb strokes my cheek
as you ask if I'm okay,
your arms take me in when I sigh.

You flip a switch for stars to appear
on your ceiling, telling me that you're
still here. You'll be here as long as I
need.

Perhaps I don't need you,
but I want this.
I want to feel this safe when I am this
vulnerable.

Mesquite – *for my grandmothers*

Both of my grandmothers are made of
mesquite roots. they have dug
themselves into the ground so deeply
the earth could not move them,
even if it tried.

the world thinks they are too rough.

Better to be taken down, used for
firewood.
when they burn, they glow like the sun,
pushing its way through clouds,
To be seen. To be heard.

Both of my grandmothers make it hard
to see the good, yet they are good.
and, maybe they make fires
so that we may be kept warm.

I Am Not Holy

My hands are not holy,
they do not hold the sacred
with enough kindness—
they were made to hold
the roughed up and worn out
shoulders of the mountain.
There is nothing holy
about my arms.
They hold the ending close,
suffocating the air with fire
to leave no trace
of the roots that crafted
the place called paradise.
This mouth is unholy.
Stained with sin, and I weep.
and I weep.
and I do not have much left in me
but the tears that find a way
to plant themselves
in the dirt, where something begins to
grow.

Maybe, that is Holy.
Maybe, that is Sacred.

I Fold Myself into a Gentle Love — *for my baby, Cruz*

My son is humming along to
Ry Cuming's "Always Remember Me"
in the car
and it makes me want to cry
because the song is soft enough
for my baby to find comfort in.

I want to be so, so very soft and gentle.
Then, there are moments when
my son is yelling and grabbing
at my arms
trying to make a jungle gym
out of me.

Two songbirds, I stand next to him
holding out my arms
and swaying us into the guitar strings,
how sweet it is to be here.

Cheyenne Raine

My Own Shadow – *for Alexis*

I am not your yellow sunlight.
I am silver moonbeams,

fishnet tights under faded denim,
heavy boots and black socks,
thin flannels with a lace bralette,
tattoos and short hair,

I'm not your light,
I'm my own shadow and darkness.

Time Is a Silent Thief

I braid my hair while you piece
together a puzzle and ask me for help
by saying mamá repeatedly.
I cry after you've gone to sleep
because time is stealing
these precious moments from me.
I do everything I can to celebrate
the puzzle being completed.
the first time you walked.
the moment you learned to knock.
and every other second
I can steal away.

Cheyenne Raine

Prayer

I am invited to pray
with a dear friend of mine,
and I cannot hold the prayer correctly.

My lips tremble in shame.
I haven't gone to church in over a year,
I suppose I'm still wondering
what God wants
from a woman like me, I suppose I think
existing is enough
and raising a good human while
learning how to embrace myself
is enough, too.

At night I do not pray,
I kiss my son on his cheek, tuck him in
with a grey blanket his madrina gifted
and close my door to eat
while a horror film
plays on the television.

In the morning I turn off my alarm
and roll out of bed, a prayer sits at the
edge of the bed, always patient.

What I Miss About Guitar Strings

I still think about guitar strings,
a little too often, if I'm honest.

Mostly, I miss swaying side to side
in the middle of my room.
even better, in the backyard!
— the fireflies swayed
with me. Me, who does not know
how to dance, but who tries
to let the sound move me,
with direction and intention.
A flow from a series of notes
I wish I knew how to sing
to the bones in my body,
back and forth in the grass.

So, maybe, I will ask you
to play your guitar a little longer
(and pull you into me).

Cheyenne Raine

Fists Full of Flowers

I will rise,
my fists full of flowers
and my soul full of light.
Isn't it the gentlest of things
that show the most strength?
Where the blossoms push through dirt
and the sun illuminates the dark—
there, you will find me.

Charmer

My lover
is a charmer.

He comes up behind me
and wraps his arms around me,
kisses my neck
while I hum along to Kenny Chesney

he is a country song
when we are together.

Cheyenne Raine

What Can You Handle?

I cringe. shudder. stare in disbelief.
when someone tells me that God.
or the universe.
will only give me what I can handle.

What I can handle?
Let me take a step back real quick.
What do you mean,
what I can handle? I ask them.
I was abused. for years.
how is that something the stars or God
decided to give to me?
As if it were a gift.
Then, they tell me, but look!
at how you've used your voice!
You've shared your story. Your healing.

I am caught off guard and dumbfounded.
Are they really telling me that my abuse
happened for a reason, and that reason
was so that I could be here today
to speak up about abuse?
No, that can't be what they mean.
that can't be how they understand
this violence. this trauma.

What about those who didn't survive?
Did the Creator or creation give them
what they couldn't handle?

Did the Creator or creation wish for
them to hurt with their last breath?
What about those who are forced into
trafficking, what about those
whose lives are threatened? What about
children? What about those who have no
voice. the poor. the disabled.
the mentally ill.

Is this what they can handle?
Is this why it happened?
No. No, I don't think so.
I know they are trying to comfort me,
to make me feel as if there is some
meaning to be found in the midst of my
healing.
But this isn't a trauma I face alone.
there are so many others.
each case different and unnecessary.
Instead, I tell them that privilege, power,
and oppressive structures are what
happened to me. They're what happen to
countless lives.
All we can do is use our voices to reclaim
our safety. to reclaim our sacredness. to
take back the nights we wander alone
with the moon. to take back the time we

Cheyenne Raine

spend alone. to take back our sense of
confidence and ourselves.
to reclaim ourselves.

Maybe, next time, tell me
that this injustice is deafening and
violent.
But my voice is strong and my healing
and resilience is proof that it has not
won. it will not win.

If This Poem Finds You

If this poem finds you
while you are scanning a bookstore
for my name and you open up
to this particular page
I hope you play "Love You Less"
by Kevin Garrett and you learn it
on your guitar.

I hope you ask
your gym to add me to their newsletter
and one day I see your photo
alongside an announcement that
you finished your last fight strong
and they're proud of you and your
progress.
I'm proud of you, too,
I'll think to myself
while reading my email.

I hope you drive past 2am and find
a stretch of road that the moon guides
— hope you count all the good things
you've gathered with each mile

and if
you happen to find this poem
I hope you find a storyteller
instead of a poet, because I can't
untangle you from my books

and all someone else will know is that
you were / are / continue to be important
to me.

If this poem finds you,
I think a simple phone call to say that
you are listening to Seaforth tonight
is another poem waiting to happen.

I've Always Been Ready to Leave or Be Left

It's not my best quality
but I've always been ready.
Maybe it's a response I default to
after my trauma. it can be that, right?
That I won't be too attached, won't
be too invested.

If you leave, I might need a day or so to
bounce back, but I'll be fine. If I leave, I
might need a week to mourn my loss.
I'll be okay.

I know you hate when I say I'm okay,
but, really, I am. I hope you believe me.
This is something I'm ready for.

Still,
I could unlearn it, I think. I could be
ready to stay. to remain with someone
who treats me and their life in the best
of ways.

Exposing the Not-So-Tender Part of My Soul

You will think I am stupid
for apologizing that I am not soft
(enough).
you will think: Yes. yes, you are.
I will be gracious (enough),
I would say, "thank you for telling me
that I have hidden my coarseness well.
I hope to remain gentle, for you."

You will find a bare piece of my soul.
Exposed (in a raw form) without
an ounce of tenderness. thick mud.
hot, dry sand that stings after
it has been blown into your face
for two hours. (A sandstorm.)
I hope. I hope. I hope.
that you will be okay. with my heavy.
with my rough. with my aggressive.
with my weather-beaten bones.

An Apartment for My Octobers

I paint the furniture burnt orange
and string up lights around the
apartment,
home is what I make it
and I make it feel like Octobers
I revel in. I've gathered dried pampas
grass to set in brown glass jars placed
on shelves and I've tossed out any trace
of sadness. any trace of spring.
My friend stops by for dinner and curls
up on the couch with me,
I tell her that the room is almost
complete.
Perhaps I am missing a bookshelf
for my poems.

Even if this home is briefly mine,

I will stretch my arms out in every inch
and celebrate my Octobers.

When You Need to Know

When your nose is stuck
in between crisp pages
and your heart
is melting with the honey
that is stirred into your tea,
that is when you know
          you know
that things will come together
softly. slowly. sweetly.
(I look at you with love
and awe. Do not forget that.)

Time Is Soft

You deserve
early mornings,
sunrises
to pour past
your curtains,
the kind of light
that kisses you
and reminds you
that time is soft.

Cheyenne Raine

Trusting Rough Hands

You will laugh,
at how I place
fallen constellations
into your rough hands.
You will laugh
and ask if I trust you
with delicate things.

Yes. yes. a thousand times:
yes. / If you crush them,
they will stain your fingers
and they will still
be as lovely as they were
before I picked them
from the midnight sky /
yes. I trust you
with the most fragile
of things: the stars. the sky,
the sun, and me.

They Will Ask You What It Felt Like to Be a Poem

They will ask you what it felt like
to be the poem / the book / the story.

Truthfully, I think you will say
it was as simple as existing.
that you had no idea existing
was a poem in itself,
maybe you felt seen or held
or maybe it was nothing.
Maybe it was a quiet unfolding.

They will wonder if I saw something
special in you or
something breath-taking.
I didn't. I don't. You're just as human
as anyone else.
and everyone becomes a poem
when you share a fleeting moment
of this lifetime together.

Cheyenne Raine

I Don't Care How Long It Takes to Get Back to Me

He no longer calls me honey
and that is alright.
I turn up the music in my car
and roll down the windows,
sing so loud I think the cars
passing by on the highway
know. Traveling to ease the pain.
it's not so much that I miss him.
more so that I miss me.

I miss me.

I wish I knew where to go
to make a home out of the leaving
and the arriving
and I want to know how to make a song
feel like a second chance.
Cars passing me by know. they know.

I have to get back to me.

The Light in an Afterglow

Horizons

There are horizons
I have yet to trace.
There are mountain ranges
I have yet to climb.
There are skies
I have yet to capture.
There is a whole world
I have yet to discover.

Tin Roof

You are not asking for vacancies,
empty places to hide and dwell in.
You are not asking
for a roof that is barely a home.
(The tapping of rainwater on tin,
the way a storm makes the house
shake—your body included.)

You are not asking for air.
A deep breath of oxygen
that is exhaled moments later
as a new mixture.
You are asking for strength.
You are asking for patience.

You are not asking for a roof
that falls apart
when the sun is too much
(Too much to sit under.
Too much to run below.
Too much to look at).

You are asking for a song
that yells and kicks.
A song that asks your skeleton
to pull itself together, to be strong
for one more lifetime. one more.

Cheyenne Raine

A song that builds a foundation
and sets a tin roof
above your head.

The Way the Stars Do

I wonder if you notice any stars in my
eyes, any hint of beauty in my smile.
I aspire to embody healing. or, maybe,
to embody light.
Someone that radiates a tenderness,
the kind that is found in cotton pillows
and herbal teas with a spoonful of honey.
I wonder if you would ever know
that I carry a pain. a hurt in my chest,
and some nights and mornings
are worse than others.
maybe you wouldn't.
I suppose it's difficult, there's nothing
to show the trauma.
it hides under my skin.
I wonder if you realize that I am still me.
I am still capable of silliness and
laughter,
of nurturing and blooming,
of bursting into a galaxy
of endless light.
I think I could be that.

I wonder if I could point out the places
where I felt safest
and where I felt the most confident.

Cheyenne Raine

Where I felt the most peace and where I
could almost forget everything, except
the way the stars glittered in the sky,
wishing that my eyes could glitter
the way they did. the way they do.

You Are the Lighthouse –
for Regan

Calling out to me
are the endless trees lining
my path home
from an Ohio sunset that welcomed me
with a storm
brewing to the right of my car window.

I've spent twenty-four hours,
give or take, with you
and feel an overwhelming sense of
gratitude
as we are two birds of the same feather,
gasping at the sight of peach clouds
stacked on top of each other,
an endless effort to reach
the golden globe sinking
into the highways and farmlands.

This place is unfamiliar,
yet, you are the lighthouse,
rays of excitement beaming
in an embrace – our first touch –
a day that feels like opening up and
smells of fresh beginnings.
the rain is quiet on the windows in your
home.

Cheyenne Raine

we watch the sun leave a trail of kisses
against the underbelly of the clouds
providing room for the rain to hold a
sacred space for us.

To Grow, Again

Heavy rains
after a drought,
now, I am able
to grow, again.
to truly thrive.

Cheyenne Raine

To Wear the Golden Crown

Summer I
For the sun
to place a golden crown
on my head,
I must release
the grief.
But it digs into my chest
and demands for more.
Give me wings. Give me flight.
s o m e t h i n g. please.
The hurt melts against my skin
and it does not wash away
when the sun's rays shower
themselves across my body.

Autumn
The ache makes me rotten. bitter.
my leaves. my blossoms.
falling into the dirt.
I have no room for the sun.
My branches slouch and tilt.
My tears dry up on my cheeks,
staining my face with a sadness
that does not know how to quiet down,
it seeps into the roots and I haven't the
words to tell someone. anyone.
that the sun has left me alone.

Winter
All is quiet. a scab on my right arm.
covered by layers of wool, hidden.
where the sun cannot find me.

The beauty has become dull,
my pulse a faint throbbing.
Does the sun see me?
Is there still time to rewrite the end?
These roots are still my own.
The rain still quenches my thirst.
Perhaps. perhaps this is the waiting,
waiting for the wound to mend.

Spring
My eyes!
They have never been so full
of rivers. they flow, I am a spring.
I sprout with change and the beginning
of a healing narrative. to be hopeful,
to see the sun.
The sun and its warmth.
My eyes, they have never been
so full of light.
The earth takes big gulps
of my tears, savoring
the freshwater spring.

Summer II
For the sun
to place a golden crown
on my head,
I must be here.
I must simply exist.
despite the autumn.
despite the winter.
despite the spring.
I have no need for wings,
I am everything I have always needed.

I Was the Night

I was the night sky
in your bruised chest:
here, there are no tears.
here, there is no pain.
here, the sun rises
and hope is tangible.

Cheyenne Raine

Such Gentleness

Always, there is an after
that I haven't held
in my hands.
but I have walked on it
with my bare feet / truly.
it was filled with sand
and steps made of marble.
warm grains spilling down
the empty staircase.
I was gifted silence
and a song poured past
my lips, with such gentleness.
I ask myself how
am I to be soft,
when I have only known
the sand stuck to my soles?

You say, "like this. just like this."
(The sun slumbers, as you tuck it
into my black hair, behind my ear.)

A New Risk – *for Karina*

There's something exciting
about leading you to
new landscapes and places,
trying new restaurants
and new adventures;
always, I am bringing you
to open up your mind
and give in to the risk.

The Woman I Want to Be

I want to be good for me.

I want my bones to shake when I speak
my truth. I want my wounds to heal
when I cry. I want my soul to breathe
when I touch the ocean. I want my lips
to open when I taste the moonlight.

I want to become a woman who does not
apologize for her overflow of creativity.
I want to be all I need.

I want to embrace every emotion and
learn the language of my body's needs
and wants and aspirations.
I want to be able to dance with myself,
without worrying what the next step is.
I want to be my own, always. I want to
dress up in red lipstick and black heels, I
want to let my soul go free.

I never want to return to yesterday's
arms.

I will push forward,
with storms in my chest.

Ohio and Everything After

It's been a long time coming, but
I'm ready.
I'm ready for a long road trip alone.
I'm ready for my baby's toddler years.
I'm ready for more bills, better bills,
bills that mean I'm moving up and on.
I'm ready for a campfire.
I'm ready for a love that feels timeless.
I'm ready for a company
I can grow with.
I'm ready to start.
Ready to embrace the forks in the road.

What Afterglows Feel Like

I feel like hiking for five hours
and coming home to cook lemon
spaghetti with zucchini,
a new favorite dish of mine,
a love language to my tongue
and my stomach.

I feel like learning Muay Thai and
allowing my body to become
a weapon I can trust and find comfort in.
I want to look in the mirror and
see a woman.
who is a gun. who is a knife.

I feel like writing poetry
when I don't have words
to share with her,
treat a poem like a habit,
a healthy one that my therapist told me
I could learn to grow.
Like the potted basil
I water on the patio.

Sometimes the afterglow feels like
working.
sometimes it feels like living.
other times it is watching the sun
climb into my bedroom at 7am.

Lemon Sun

Holding a lemon sun
while squinting my eyes

smiling
at the touch of the wind
brushing through my hair,
waves of dark brown playing
with the heat

running with the wild horses
that live behind the ranch
I used to visit every weekend or so,
telling them
to return, tomorrow.

Letters to the Night

Dear Dusk,
I trust you. it's taken me a while to meet
you half-way. I wasn't sure that I would
ever be comfortable with you, again. but,
here we are.

Dear Moon,
I apologize for staying indoors as you
rose. Tonight, I've decided to open up
the door. I've decided that it's time I let
your silver light touch my smile, again.

Dear Stars,
I'm ready to trace patterns in your vast
array of gold. I'm ready to rest my head
in the grass and whisper wild tales that
fit into your constellations.

Dear Night,
For all you are, I will not mix you up
with someone who stole my sense of
safety while you were filling the sky
with dark blue and purple.

Dear Night,
I'm learning to fall in love with you,
once more. You sing me to sleep and
wrap me up in grey watercolors.

All the hours you give to me. all the new
beginnings you offer. all the skies, the
open, vast and wild possibilities.

Dear Night, I'm with you.

Cheyenne Raine

I Send the Gift of Petals –
for Theresa

I will always gift you flowers.
I will never not want you to feel
surrounded
by the nectar of colorful lilies.
I will never not want you to inhale
the scent of honeysuckles.
I will always want your home to be full
of warmth and things that blossom.

I will always gift you the dream
of maroon-soaked sunsets
and rose-tinted dawns,
places to exist in such bliss.

I will always delight in your existence,
the dazzling display of light dancing
in my eyes.
you are a gift to me.

I Am Mine

I am everything I need.
I am everything I want.
All I can dream is what I can achieve.
All I can achieve is what I can honor.
All I can honor is who I am.
I am this fire on the horizon.
I am this glowing hope.
I am the art piece. I am the artist.
I am the rainfall and the storm.
I am mine.

Cheyenne Raine

I Could Have an Afterglow

I think I could have an afterglow
once you finish listening to my story
and I wipe the tears away, maybe
you would see it.

like a neon sign that buzzes
in the midnight air. Yes,
much like that.
I am not lonely, I don't think.
Simply waiting for a moment
to push me into the deep end
of the waters.
as if the trauma could be outrun.

as if it wasn't a part of me.

The Place You Chose to Exist (With Me)

You're standing in the doorway
with all you have ever had
and I don't know
quite why your journey
has led you to me
but I tell you to come inside
and rest a while, lay your belongings
down in the hallway until you decide
whether this is a place you could
breathe or a place you will
remember to begin with.

I filled the space with noise
and words, with warmth and
a soft blanket against the cold.
You closed your eyes
and said it had been so long
since you stopped to exist,
so that's what we did.

We existed in between.

Cheyenne Raine

Underneath the Same Sky

You are looking at the same moon that
I see. I am looking at the same sun
that you see.
I am watching the night, as it collects
shadows of lavender and maroon
dreams.
you are watching the sun, as it begins
to rise, coloring the sky with scarlet and
peach hues. You are soaking in every
shade the sky experiences and I am miles
away, wondering:
How magnificent does the view look
from your apartment window?

San Antonio Riverwalk

The Riverwalk is high school memories,
singing on a boat and playing my
violin—
I haven't seen my violin in years.

I went on a date and the man told me
that he found the Riverwalk fascinating,
I think it's okay.
Maybe that's what I need though,
to leave San Antonio and come back
and realize that this city has gems
within.

The date went well and I ended up not
hearing anything from him again, still, I
hope the Riverwalk treats him well
when Christmas and Fiesta come to the
city, the noise and the people will never
cease to amaze me.

Waiting to Be Found

You have untouched rivers
below your heart strings.
You have abandoned cathedrals
waiting to be found.
One day, the stars will create
a thin line to you, and I will
follow it through.

I will return to myself, one day.

Tell Me How This Feels

Tell me how it feels to laugh
so hard you start to cry and lose your
breath.
tell me how it feels to cry
until there is no more water
in your body.
tell me how it feels to be so focused
on winning that the sidelines
become blurry
but you can still hear your name
being shouted with pride.

Tell me if it's worth it.
This relationship with work and life,
with mind and body,
between ice cold baths
and waking up at 6am to see the sunrise.

Tell me how this feels, sharing
a bottle of beer while the summer air
rolls in.

Cheyenne Raine

Blooming, Despite

I am made of something
that blooms
despite the winter moons.
despite the empty clouds,
imagine the lack of rain
falling on lips made of petals.
despite the dryness of the dirt.
despite the cold
that does not leave my shoulders.

Little root of a rose
bearing thorns—notice
how I make room for myself.
notice how I soften for the sky.

What We Deserve

I think we deserve
something softer
than the bitter winds
that society has blown
against our skin.
I think we deserve
something sweeter
than the bitter taste
of our own blood
spilling from open wounds.

I think there must be something more
out there / out where the sky sets /
something that brings us to our knees
and says: Yes, yes, I know the weight
is burdensome,
but you are safe. you are safe.
you are safe.

Poems to Remind Us of Hope

We need more soft poems.
the kind that take you to a place
where nothing hurts. a haven of sorts,
an abandoned kingdom with
hallways full of sunlight.
The things I could tell you
about this kingdom. our kingdom.
our safe place, our safe poem.

We would greet every stranger without
wondering if they would or might hurt
us. we would spend more time in the
gardens, with books in our hands,
unaware of our surroundings.
We would drink for fun
and we wouldn't worry about the time
or the path we'd use to get home.
in our kingdom. in our poem.

Why can't that be now?
Why can't our soft poem begin here?
Why can't our hopes take bloom with
us, in this space, in this time?

We need more poems that carry hope
and poems that don't beg for the sun to
come up, because we are too busy
admiring the moon and all of her
elegance.

Maroon Daydreams

We need more poems that heal
and more poems that gather up the
remains
of our pain, using the soil to harvest
new beginnings.
Soft poems. Safe poems.
Poems that remind us
that we must love and love and love.

Afterword

by Regan Noelle Smith, author of
Morning Air, Morning Light

With vulnerability and strength,
Cheyenne has not only walked through,
but re-lived each element of *Maroon
Daydreams*—letting us into her world of
experience and healing.

Throughout her healing journey, we see
a raw and honest self-love shine through.
And in her every day journey, she
depicts a present-state beauty. We see
this through her motherhood moments,
times with tea, or a single second with a
loved one. This is the most prolific
theme I have pulled from reading this
collection—that the tiny moments that
make up our day are the ones to be
treasured the most. Our past is
comprised of these puzzle pieces that
web together our experience, not just the
peaks and the valleys.

Cheyenne has created a collection of
poems that walks us, hand-in-hand,

through the remembrance of past trauma. She takes us through her healing journey that's intertwined with motherhood and finding new love. We see her religious convictions wrapped throughout, as she continues to heal and grow into new spaces.

This book is as gentle yet as unrelenting as a heartbeat: always choosing to see beauty within the current moment, while seeking out healing and truth. It is truly a delightful first read, and it continues to speak in relevant ways every time I re-read it. The publication and republication of *Maroon Daydreams* is truly a gift to any reader who has hurts they are still healing.

This unrelenting awareness of beauty in the present moment is what *Maroon Daydreams*, and Cheyenne's poetry, has inspired within me time and time again. I hope this is what you have also found through this collection: that even the minutia moments are monumental.

About the Author

Photography by Christy Anna

Cheyenne Raine, co-owner of Raine and Rose Co., lives in the San Antonio light, pulling warmth into her creative life. She is a mother of one and a cheerleader to many business owners. With an ever-present cup of tea steeping in her hand, she brings a fierce heart to every minute of her full schedule. Her poetry book publications include *Maroon Daydreams, Charcoal Thunderstorms* and *Lemon Acuarelas.*

Find her at teawithraine.com

Raine &
Rose Co.

Serving women who celebrate their
work as a *passion project*.

Co-owners, Cheyenne Raine and
Theresa Sopko Ressa, work with the
Raine and Rose Co team to craft
websites, marketing strategies, books,
and brand identities for creative business
owners while also prioritizing a healthy
work and life balance for everyone
involved in Raine and Rose projects.

Learn more at raineandrose.co

www.ingramcontent.com/pod-product-compliance
Lightning Source LLC
Chambersburg PA
CBHW072350090426
42741CB00012B/2995

* 9 780578 387765 *